MW01243288

PERSEVERANCE

AS A MEANS TO

OVERCOME

YOUR LIFE'S

OBSTACLES

HOW I DID IT AND HOW YOU CAN TOO!

SANDER A. FLAUM

NEW YORK, NY

Copyright © 2022 by Sander A. Flaum.

All rights reserved. No part of this book may be reproduced in any written, electronic, recording, or photocopying without written permission of the publisher or author. The exception would be in the case of brief quotations embodied in articles or reviews and pages where permission is specifically granted by the publisher or author.

Flaum Navigators, Inc.
Perseverance as a Means to Overcome Your Life's Obstacles
630 Park Avenue, Ste 9B
New York, NY 10065
Printed in the United States of America

Although every precaution has been taken to verify the accuracy of the information contained herein, the author and publisher assume no responsibility for any errors or omissions. No liability is assumed for damages that may result from the use of information contained within.

Perseverance as a Means to Overcome Your Life's Obstacles
Sander A. Flaum -- 1st ed.

CONTENTS

This book is dedicated to my beautiful and late wife, Mechele, who died in November 2017.
We had a wonderful life together. She was inspiring, supportive and the most loving person I have ever known. May she rest in peace.

Also, to my loyal Chief of Staff of 20 years, Lisa Pollione.

OTHER BOOKS BY SANDER A. FLAUM

The 100-Mile Walk

Big Shoes

The Best Thing That Could Ever Happen to You

Boost Your Career

The Stutter Steps

Benign Paranoia

PERFECTLY FLAWED

A STUTTER IS INDICATIVE OF ONLY ONE THING: A person who stutters.

Nervousness does not cause stuttering. People who stutter are no more fearful, anxious, or shy than anyone else. Stuttering cannot be caught by hearing another person stutter. There is no link whatsoever between stuttering and intelligence.

In fact, some of the most successful, accomplished people throughout history have struggled with this often misunderstood condition—people like Claudius, Winston Churchill and King George VI to President Joe Biden. There are business leaders: the late Jack Welch from General Electric, Home Depot's Arthur Blank, and journalists such as John Stossel, formerly of *20/20*. Stutterers have found fame and fortune in occupations that don't rely on speaking abilities, such as athletes Greg Louganis and Tiger Woods and writers like Lewis Carroll and John Updike. Others like Elvis Presley, Mel Tillis, and Carly Simon, worked through their disability in song. Actors like Samuel L. Jackson, Emily Blunt, Bruce Willis, James Stewart, and Marilyn Monroe faced their stuttering head on.

According to the Stuttering Foundation of America, one percent of the population stutters, and four times as many males as females stutter.

There are many theories about the cause of stuttering. Is it a physical issue? A psychological problem? Or is something else altogether? There is a growing belief that stuttering is rooted in genetic as well as neurological and physiological causes. Emily Blunt, who serves on the American Institute for Stuttering (AIS) board of directors, notes that her uncle, cousin, and grandfather also stuttered.

Some sort of weakness in linguistic encoding along with motor production may be associated with stuttering onset. There may be emotional factors as well. Some experts believe the problem of stuttering in school children and adults can be a coping strategy. Recent research indicates that genetics, neuromuscular development, and a child's environment, including family dynamics, all play a role in the onset of stuttering.

I believe my stuttering is a result of both.

One thing I know for sure is that stutterers tend to avoid eye contact, words that trip us up, and social settings where we might have to talk to strangers. We do whatever we can, including using "um" and "ah," to get through our stuttering, and those avoidance methods become habits.

The psychological aspects stem from our efforts to avoid negative reactions, the shame and embarrassment, as well as frustrations we feel. This component leads us to self-defeating thoughts and actions, such as turning down jobs or promotions that require more face-to-face meetings with co-workers or clients. Most stutterers deal with more than their fair share of adversity.

I'm ashamed to admit that when my kids were young, a neighborhood teenager my daughter knew pulled up alongside our car. At the stop light, he began mocking the way Pamela spoke.

I got out of the car, punched him right in the face, got back in the car, and drove off. Not my finest moment.

Joe Biden talked openly during the 2020 Presidential Campaign about his lifelong struggle with stuttering, which he still deals with, especially when working long hours on the campaign trail. "It has nothing to do with your intelligence quotient. It has nothing to do with your intellectual makeup," he said during a CNN Town Hall appearance.

Biden said he stays in touch with about fifteen others who stutter. They encourage each other, and he tells them, it is "critically important for them not to judge themselves by their speech – and to not let that define them."

While Biden and every one of these household names overcame their limitations, I can promise you it wasn't easy. People not only believe the myths out there about stuttering but can be, and often are, judgmental and cruel to those of us who struggle to get their words out.

I was determined to never let this impediment stand in my way. My story is one of overcoming and becoming the person I was determined to become. While my particular challenge was that of stuttering and stammering as a person in the world of public relations, marketing, and advertising, I believe the struggle and desire to be accepted is universal.

No matter what you face, and we all face something, I offer my story.

I did it, and you can too.

PART I
WALKING THE WALK

YOU SHOULD TALK

I WAS BORN ON APRIL 5, 1937, THE ELDEST CHILD of Joseph and Rose Flaum, a Jewish couple from Brooklyn, New York. Four years later, my sister Adele came along.

A happy, harmonious family we were not, but we got by.

My father, Joseph Flaum, worked for his father at Flaum's Appetizing, a fine food purveyor in Brooklyn that specialized in retail and wholesale Kosher foods such as lox, herring, pickles, spreads, dips, herring, and other delicious Jewish heritage products. He spent his life working seventy-five hour weeks. Needless to say, I didn't see him much. He provided for us but was exhausted when he dragged himself through the apartment door at night after serving customers, cutting fish, and hauling pickle barrels. His life was devoted to pleasing his father, and he was never able to realize any of his dreams. He went to college for one year until he was pulled out by his father to work at the family business.

As a result, or maybe because it's just the way he was, my father was a nice enough guy but lacked a personality, and he lacked much in the way of meaningful parenting skills. That job fell to my mother, Rose. Thankfully, she did it with brains and grace.

I needed her wit and wisdom because when I was five and started to speak, it became apparent that I both stuttered and stammered. Stuttering typically starts early in life but disappears in 80% of cases within three or four years.

Mine did not.

YESHIVA

I STARTED OFF IN AN ORTHODOX JEWISH SCHOOL.
We spent our mornings learning Hebrew and afternoons doing
our coursework in English. A school day ran nine hours, and the
pace of the Hebrew recitation brought my stuttering to light.

There was some teasing amongst the kids, but they were kind
enough to do it behind my back. I was popular and a good athlete
thanks to my Uncle Maury who taught me to play baseball. My
parents had little money, but my Aunt Terry made sure that I was
the best dressed boy at school by buying me all of my clothes, often
from Saks Fifth Avenue.

The Russian immigrant rabbis of the old-world Brooklyn
Yeshiva did their best, but their best did not include being patient
or kind with me. I knew the answers, but when I couldn't get them
out quickly enough, I was shamed in front of the class. One rabbi
was particularly impatient when I couldn't get words out. He'd ask
a question, and if I couldn't get the words out because of my stuttering, he'd slap me on the hand with a ruler, spank me, or even
worse, use a belt on my back.

My grandfather was a huge supporter of the yeshiva and came in every Friday with cash that added up to half the rabbis' weekly salary. I watched him hand out that cash to those men, knowing how brutal they were to me. I quickly developed a loathing for school, and soon, the rabbis were having to drag me inside.

They treated me worse as a result.

PORKY PIG

ALONG WITH THE RABBIS, I COUNTED PORKY PIG as a major nemesis—yes, the popular cartoon character beloved by many. While the younger generations may know Porky mostly from his more recent appearances in the *Space Jam* movies and *The Looney Tunes Show* on Cartoon Network, he's been around since the 1930s and is one of the top cartoon characters in history.

The Commodore Theatre was next to my grandfather's store in Brooklyn. On Sunday afternoons, I went there with my friends for an action-packed double feature—a John Wayne war movie and a Hopalong Cassidy western or whatever was playing that week. The movies were usually separated by a Walter Lantz cartoon.

Every Sunday, I prayed the cartoon wouldn't show Porky Pig, but since he was the big money maker in the 40s and 50s, it almost always was.

Why did I hate that particular cartoon character so much?

Porky Pig was known for his severe stutter. Not only did he stutter his way through the cartoon, but he was often featured in the final moments offering his signature line, *Th-th-th-that's all folks!*

Every time it happened, I felt the eyes of my buddies peering at me, sharing my embarrassment and horror at Porky's painful speech patterns.

My friends didn't laugh, but the other movie patrons howled every time Porky's face turned red trying to speak! For many, he was a beloved character, but when I heard him stutter away, I wanted to crawl under my seat.

He sounded just like me.

SPEECH THERAPY

CURRENT RESEARCH SAYS NOT TO PUT PRESSURE ON speech if you have a stuttering child because the speech patterns will often resolve on their own. In those days, however, my concerned mother made sure I went to every speech therapy program she could find. She even scraped together what she could for a program across town via two bus transfers and a train at the National Hospital for Speech Disorders. Given that their primary method was to teach people how to live with their stutter, it really didn't help.

I hated the fact that stuttering was an obstacle I could not easily fix.

It certainly didn't help that my grandfather was embarrassed by my stutter and was dismissive of me because of it. When my dad would take me to his father's apartment for a visit or with him to work, he would worry about his flawed son and coach me the whole way over to "talk slowly" over and over.

At least he wasn't forgetting about me. That happened too. On one memorable occasion, we changed clothes early, while it was still Shabbat, crossed Broadway to escape from the people we knew, and got into Harold Kandel's car to set off for an afternoon at the racetrack. After my dad and his pal finished watching and betting on the races, he and Harold took off without me. I was the only one left in the place when my dad finally remembered that he had brought me along. He came back to get me, but that didn't exactly help me feel important to him.

Thankfully, while my dad was preoccupied with work and leisure distractions unrelated to his son, Mom was organizing various therapies and telling me there was nothing wrong with me; I was just different. My uncle Maury was a bad stutterer. He was also quite a genius and a very successful music composer and arranger. When he needed someone to write his books, my mom stepped up and took on that responsibility for him.

That's how Rose Flaum was a wonderful role model. She often spoke about doing the right thing—looking for the ways that each of us can tap the fount of integrity within us and channel our efforts towards others. She provided the spark I needed. If someone loved me enough to turn her life upside down for me, assuring me that I was well worth the effort, I might as well believe too.

Because of her, I decided early on that even after going through every kind of speech therapy program known to man (mom was not a quitter) that this was *not* going to be a handicap for me. I could not permit my stuttering to be an impediment to my personal aspirations.

Most days, I handled it well. On the other days, the days I was frustrated or down, Mom would say, "You're just going to have to work harder and be smarter than your competitors in life, and you'll do well."

Smarter and harder, I repeated like a mantra until it became one.

14

BAR MITZVAH

ONE DAY, MOM LOOKED AT MY BACK AND NOTICED a scar from one of the rabbi's belts. She knew they'd been tough on me, and in those days, things were slightly different, but that was the final straw. Despite my grandfather's huge support for the school, she wasn't going to allow them to abuse me anymore. Against the strident objections of my father and my grandfather, Rose withdrew me and enrolled me in a nearby public school.

My grandfather continued to pay the rabbis every Friday, and my family and I were all but disowned, the fact of which was highlighted after my mom planned a beautiful celebration for me at Knapp's Mansion. Her friends, my friends, and the family had all been invited. Two weeks before the event, my grandfather pulled the money out saying, "I just can't do it."

He gave no further explanation, but we all knew it was because he was furious at me and my mom for taking me out of Yeshiva. Never mind that I'd been abused by the rabbis or that it wasn't the right place for me, or that I was just a kid trying to make his way in the world. His image in our tightknit community was much more important to him.

Undaunted, my mother arranged for the celebration to be held in my aunt's apartment, up in the Bronx, instead. It was an example to me about how there's always a way around a seemingly insurmountable situations.

Because my grandfather was ultra-Orthodox, we attended a temple where the women didn't sit with the men. On the day of the bar mitzvah, he came to shul and sat in the front row. I don't know whether it was nerves, his presence, or a combination of both, but I went up to recite my Torah portion and lost my voice. I got the words out without stuttering or stammering, but no one could hear me. I was so hoarse; I could only speak in a whisper.

My grandfather was in the front row, and I could not find my voice—a total disaster.

I hated that I had proved him right. The image of standing up there on the bima with no voice haunted me for years.

Later, I realized he was just unkind and unfeeling in general. When he died, he had arranged to be buried in Israel. When my grandmother died, however, he'd made no such arrangement for her. She was buried in the local cemetery in Brooklyn, thousands of miles away from the Holy Land and her husband. He hadn't bothered to have his own wife buried beside him.

What a guy!

PUBLIC SCHOOL

"SANDER, I WANT THAT COLORED PENCIL," SAID ONE of my new classmates at public school.

"I'm sorry. I'm using it now," I responded.

"You fucking Jew. Why'd you kill Christ?" he said in response. I punched him as hard as I could.

When the final bell rang at day's end, I walked out of school, and there were three guys out there waiting for me. They beat the hell out of me and broke my nose for the first time. It certainly wasn't the warm welcome I'd hoped for, but at least people were not punishing me for my speech impediment.

To me, it was something of a win.

Other than learning how to navigate the large pond that was public school, getting out of Yeshiva turned out to be a very positive experience. I did well in school, was a good athlete, and made plenty of friends—including my best buddy, Stan Gelber. I didn't let stuttering become a handicap that held me back.

Mostly, anyway.

At age fifteen, I began going out with this beautiful cheerleader from Midwood High School in the center of Brooklyn. I was the envy of all of my friends. She was a knockout! But, one day, I phoned her to confirm our Friday night date, and she said, "Wow, you know, the wallpaper hanger was over today, and he spoke just like you; he couldn't get a word out."

Gut-punched, I hung up, and that was the last time we spoke.

Thankfully, I had sports to distract me, and I was an avid baseball fan and played in Brooklyn's Prospect Park league. I couldn't get the "S" out of my mouth to say "Sander," so I used my middle name, Allen. I would have played every day, but I knew I had to escape the limitations of my Orthodox Jewish upbringing. To do so, I worked nights to earn money for college at Murray's Sporting Goods, where I packed and delivered cartons. It wasn't easy, but I was determined to get out of Brooklyn.

Thankfully, I had a wonderful English teacher and mentor at the Boy's High School named Richard Rampell. He really understood the challenges I faced and helped me go above and beyond any potential limitations. In fact, I had all As in high school until Mr. Rampell gave me a B on an English paper.

"I've never gotten a B," I said to him, shocked when I saw my grade.

"I know you can do better," he said.

I went home and rewrote the paper that night and gained my A.

I had other supporters on the staff as well. When I ran for high school president against the captain of the track team, we both had to get up and speak in front of the school. Mrs. Roth, a Spanish teacher who was known for being very cold and not associating with any of the students, came in through the back door as I got up in front of the auditorium. She leaned against a wall with her arms folded. When I finished, she waved, smiled at me, and left without hearing the other boy's speech. My speech wasn't very good, and the captain of the track team won the presidency handily (although I would later be voted most handsome, which made up for some of the loss), but I'll always remember her support.

I applied to and was admitted to a number of colleges, including Cornell. After working every night at Murray's Sporting Goods to pay for school; however, I was ready for some fun in my life. I was a big fan of Ohio State football, so when I was accepted at The Ohio State University, it seemed like the ideal environment to work hard and play hard as well.

Also, it seemed as far away from home as I could get.

OHIO STATE

I WAS SIXTEEN AND A HALF ON THE DAY MOM TOOK me to the Ohio State Limited train. I boarded in Brooklyn and got off in Columbus, Ohio, elated about my new life ahead.

My first goal as a Buckeye was to win a spot on the college baseball team. While the Dodgers hadn't knocked on my door with a contract, I was a good player. Ohio State had a great team, and I figured it was worth a try.

That year, they recruited the best baseball team in their history, and I got cut after pitching my third preseason game. Mom sent me six dollars a week, but without that hoped-for scholarship, I had to work different jobs in order to stay in Columbus.

Disappointed but undaunted, I made it work somehow without ever telling her I'd been cut from the team!

My favorite job during college was at Green's Clothing Store in downtown Columbus. The owners, Bob and Betty Green, were wonderful people who treated me like a son. There were no weekend meals at my fraternity, Phi Epsilon Pi, so Bob used to drive over on Saturday morning to pick me up and take me to his home for dinner.

My years at OSU were filled with joy. In fact, they were the happiest time four years of my life. I flourished academically, worked at the school newspaper as a reporter, and became a senior editor. I was also the business director of the *Sundial* humor magazine. I even got into a five-year program in which participants earned a law degree at night along with their bachelor's degree in liberal arts.

"A lawyer?" my mom said when I told her. "They talk all the time in the courtroom, and you're a stutterer. Honey, listen to me, you have to drop out of the program."

It was a hurtful reality, given how well I was doing with my stuttering during college, but good sons always listen to their mom, and I knew she was right, so I decided to pursue a degree in psychology.

My closest friend in college was Stan Gelber from back home in Brooklyn. (I convinced him to transfer from NYU to join me at OSU.) My college girlfriend was Rookie Hirsch—who, inspired by my issues with stuttering, went on to get her Ph.D. in speech therapy and eventually headed up a big clinic in Oakland. In those days, I was much less concerned about my stutter than finding elevator shoes to wear because Rookie was an inch taller than me! She was a lot of fun, a great dancer, and one of the prettiest girls on campus. We saw each other every day for a couple of years, and I loved her very much. We eventually split up after I got pneumonia and had to leave OSU for a semester.

During the summers, I worked as a waiter at the Gilbert's Hotel in the Catskill Mountains. (Think *Dirty Dancing*.) I got Stan a job as the music director, and we hung out with Louie Cohen the bellhop. It was work, work, and more work. When a waiter went in the wrong door, old Pop Gilbert would threaten him with, "The blood will run from you like it's running from the steak you dropped."

In those days, ROTC was a mandatory college course. I was in Air Force ROTC, where I received some great leadership training, but working on airplane engines and parts wasn't for me. I tried to transfer into the Army ROTC after the second year, but the Army recruiter I spoke with said, "You're a stutterer. How are you going to give orders? How are you going to say, 'Stop. Don't march into the lake?'"

So that was that.

Since I was only required to take ROTC for two years, I quit soon after. I had much better things to do with my time, such as having fun with my fraternity brothers, hanging out with Rookie, and playing third baseman on one of the intramural teams.

I graduated from Ohio State in 1958 with a check for $400 in my pocket from working as the business director of *Sundial Magazine*.

At graduation, my mom wanted to meet people on the baseball team. It was only then that I finally confessed I'd never played.

She began to cry.

"How'd you do it? How'd you do it?" she asked, wondering how I'd managed to put myself through school on my own.

I couldn't have been prouder.

UNIFORMED

COLLEGE GRADUATION COINCIDED WITH A MAJOR recession. Work was difficult to find. Although Mom helped me write a strong resume, all I got of note was a job offer as a salesman for a telephone firm in Pennsylvania.

I declined.

Finally, my cousin Stan Kissel helped me land a job in public relations for a furrier. I liked doing PR, but the company wasn't for me.

Soon after, I enlisted in the U.S. Army and was stationed in the Army Reserve at Fort Dix from 1959–1962. I loved every minute of my time there—except for the one run in I had with a fellow G.I. who was a football player from the University of Mississippi. He was a huge guy, but he made fun of my stuttering. One day, after he imitated me, I hit him as hard as I could. I wasn't putting up with that particular brand of teasing from anyone—not even a man mountain.

He didn't budge.

Of course, he hit me back. In fact, he threw me across the room and broke my nose in two places. Nevertheless, he respected me for standing up to him and later apologized.

We became friends, and he never ridiculed my speech again.

During my stint in the Army, I came home intermittently. On one notable occasion, my father, who spent my childhood secretly changing clothes on Shabbat to steal off to the racetrack, had the audacity to suggest I change out of my Army uniform in observance of the day of rest.

I left my apartment that day and didn't return for the rest of my enlistment.

Fortunately, because of my background in journalism at The Ohio State and my brief stint in PR, I was put into Public Relations for the Army. The civilian clerk for the 411th Quartermaster Corps was a fellow named Mario Puzo. One day, he stopped me and said, "I just finished writing a book, and I'd like for you to read it and give me your opinion."

"I'd love to," I said. "And I wish I could, but I don't have the time."

The book turned out to be *THE GODFATHER*...

While in the service, I ended up as a speechwriter for General Earl C. Bergquist, who had been President John F Kennedy's assistant attaché. The General took a liking to me and, after my hitch was up, recommended me to Bobby Kennedy. I later worked as his junior speechwriter when he ran for the Senate in 1964.

I wasn't as well suited for the combat aspects of being in the service as I was for writing.

During war games at Ft. Dix, I was put in command of a unit of soldiers and was to march them to a designated area. I'm happy to say that the recruiter who thought my stutter would impact my ability to communicate effectively was completely wrong. However, I have a terrible sense of direction. By not asking the sergeant serving by my side for directions, I marched my men into an atomic warzone. It was hours before the mess truck found us and in good time because we were starving, no thanks to me.

Of course, this story ripped through the camp.

On the day of my Honorable Discharge, and as my commanding officer was signing my release from service, he said, "Flaum, I understand you're being discharged today."

'Yes, sir," I said.

"It's a great day for the Army, Flaum," he retorted.

"Yes, sir," I said.

I'd learned much in the Army, especially that I was not meant to be a career soldier.

PART II
TALK IS CHEAP

RUDER & FINN

UPON MY DISCHARGE FROM THE ARMY, MY FIRST
ambition was to get into politics. Of course, you have to be a frequent public speaker to run for office and in many politically appointed positions. In my mind, having a bad stutter did not lend itself to that particular career path.

Stutterers have to weigh the pros and cons of their chosen profession in an entirely different way than fluent speakers. Many seek out careers in engineering, accounting, or the sciences, but I wanted to do something I enjoyed, and I enjoyed public relations, advertising, leadership, marketing, and communications.

It is always challenging to interview for jobs when you are a stutterer. If you are competing against a couple of other bright people who are fluent and you are stuttering your way through the interview, you're probably not getting the job. As my mother advised, "You have to worked harder and be smarter."

I worked briefly as a junior speechwriter for Bobby Kennedy upon getting out of the Army, and I wrote for Drug Trade News before I was able to land a job in 1963 at the public relations firm Ruder & Finn.

I was quickly assigned to the Philip Morris account, working on the new no-smoking guidelines. I took the project seriously, and my colleagues regarded me as an antismoking zealot. I became a water cooler outcast. But I had an epiphany: I didn't care what they thought as long as I was convinced I was doing the best job possible.

Soon after becoming a junior product manager, I had the responsibility of hiring a new member for my team. A senior vice president referred a woefully unqualified candidate, but the fellow really wanted the job. I ended up hiring him, perhaps in sympathy. As I might have expected, he was completely inadequate, much to the amusement of many of my colleagues, who took delight in recounting tales of his incompetence. The harder he tried, the more hopeless the situation became. I finally had to let him go. My lesson was to take a class in interviewing skills and to work closely with my personnel department chair when considering a new hire.

Lessons, or should I say, teachable moments, related to my stuttering seemed to play out on a regular basis, however.

While at Ruder & Finn, I did well and got transferred from one department to another. I came in one day late for a meeting because I'd been in attendance at another meeting. As I walked in, Harry L., the head of the new department, was making fun of my speech in front of the whole group.

"I can't believe this is what you do," I simply said.

Two weeks later, I got fired.

I wasn't sorry.

No matter how much money you're getting paid nor how much prestige you get from a particular job, if you're working for a jerk who mistreats you and other people, it's not worth it. You have to enjoy going to work every day, no matter how much money you're making. You have to be around the right people.

MARRIED MAN

AFTER LEAVING RUDER & FINN UNEMPLOYED, I MET a young woman named Susan at a major recruiting firm. Not only was she helping me to land my next job, but she was pretty and smart.

"Sander, all your friends are married. Some of them are already having kids," my mom counseled.

So, listening to my mom, I asked her out for a date.

A couple weeks later, I arranged for Susan to meet my mother. Rose liked Susan and thought she was pretty as well. I was impressed that she did *The New York Times* crossword in ink!

Six months later, we got married.

I was twenty-four, and she was twenty.

The day after the wedding, Susan's parents showed up at our Queens apartment without a call. It was a bad harbinger of things to come. From then on, I'd open the door on weekends, and there they were. Worse, they kept me from pursuing opportunities such as going to Washington after Bobby Kennedy won. My in-laws prevented that from happening.

STRAUS BROADCASTING GROUP

WITH EXPERIENCE AS A SPEECH WRITER, PUBLIC relations credentials, and a great reference from General Earl C. Bergquist, I went to the Straus Broadcasting Group to become the public relations director of radio station WMCA. My job there was to get press out on happenings at the station. I also wrote and booked speeches for the owner, R. Peter Straus.

At that time, WMCA was one of the most innovative radio stations in the nation. It was number one in New York City. Not only did they broadcast the first radio editorials, political endorsements, the very popular *Voice of America*, but they helped to popularize rock and roll.

And yet, Barry Gray, who did on air interviews in the afternoon used to walk into my office and say, "Hi, *pubic* relations."

He thought he was hysterical.

At that time, R. Peter Straus was married to Monica Lewinsky's mother. I felt so bad for Monica after the Bill Clinton scandal that I offered the young lady a job.

She declined.

She'd have been a great asset to the team.

Back in those days, I was exceptionally impatient. If I called a meeting for 9:00 AM, I expected everyone sitting around the conference table ready to go by 8:50 AM. In fact, the doors closed at the stroke of nine.

I liked my boss there quite a lot, but when he left, a guy named Franz A. took over. I didn't care for him much, and the feeling was apparently mutual. At that time, there were two young people who reported to me. I considered them both to be arrogant and disrespectful. Franz liked them.

They never came to meetings on time, so they found themselves locked out on more than one occasion. I wasn't going to hold up everyone else who was already there.

They thought I was taking too hard a line and complained to Franz about me. The complaint was that the meeting was scheduled to start at nine and at nine the conference room door was closed. He sided with them, arguing that I should have counseled them instead of instituting what he considered to be draconian measures.

I got fired.

At the time, Susan was pregnant with our first child.

In need of a job, and quickly, I was recruited to a Jewish foundation in Miami. I went down to Miami, to check it out, but my wife made it clear she wasn't coming along. Her parents were in New York, and remaining near them was her number one priority.

I wasn't thrilled about the opportunity, but it was the only thing I had going. I went down there and knew right away it was the wrong decision.

I came back to New York unsure what was going to happen next.

LEDERLE LABORATORIES

I CAN'T IMAGINE THERE ARE TOO MANY PEOPLE WHO
set out to be a pharmaceutical marketer or consultant, but my life
has been a series of doors opening and closing. Each iteration land-
ing me in a new and often unanticipated place.

While I was aggravated about my wife's lack of flexibility, her
insistence on remaining in New York paid off. I needed a job and
the pharmaceutical industry beckoned. At least it felt that way a
month later in 1965 when I was recruited to Lederle Laboratories
(which would later be bought out by Wyeth, and is now Pfizer) in
Pearl River, New York. As a public relations manager, it was my
job to help promote the various pharmaceuticals the company had
developed. I was twenty-six years old and suspected I was the only
liberal Democrat within the industry.

That might be why I got the job!

My very pregnant wife and I moved to Rockland County, north
of New York City, and I embarked on the next significant step in
my career.

My new job went well, and no one called me out or made fun
of my stutter—not in front of me, anyway. One day, however,

the marketing director Bob Hensel called me and said, "Sander, I know you're smart, but you give answers before the questions are even asked."

Coming up in corporate life, you're not going to get the job if you can't get your name out. I definitely had a need for people to know my point of view and understand that despite any issues I had. I knew my stuff, and I wanted them to know too. I'm sure I developed this habit as a result of my stutter.

Thankfully, Bob understood this and had a great solution. "I'm going to send you to a listening program—four days on how to keep your mouth shut and listen to all points of view before you answer."

The class turned out to be very helpful in teaching me about the value of listening to all points of view before chiming in with my own thoughts. A lot of what I learned really stayed with me for life, and I was thankful for that experience.

The course also got me thinking about further education.

After a few years in the public relations department, I realized I lacked the upward mobility I ultimately sought. In the corporate world, you didn't do anything without the sign-off from the president of the company. I felt stifled waiting for activity as opposed to looking for it and developing it on my own. I wanted to move, and there was nowhere significant for me to aspire. I couldn't go on with no real recognition other than "Sander's doing a good job, thanks," so I decided I needed to act.

Determined to make my mark, I used the GI Bill to pay for graduate school at night and on weekends. I busted my hump to attain my MBA and became valedictorian of my class at Fairleigh Dickinson University. The dean of the business school dropped a line to the president of Lederle, Bob Luciano, and let him know that one of his employees had graduated at the top of the class. I also spoke at commencement, which was almost as significant of an accomplishment.

Two weeks later, I was plucked out of public relations and found myself in in the company's management development program.

I had a wonderful time being transferred from department to department for various training periods and then ended up in marketing (where I wanted to be all along). For the next decade and a half, I kept my nose to the grindstone and worked my way up through the ranks of product manager and group product manager to director of marketing.

HOLLINS INSTITUTE

I WAS MY EARLY THIRTIES WHEN I SAW A MAN ON TV who suffered from a severe lifelong stutter. He had had found success by attending a newly opened program at the Hollins Communications Research Institute (HCRI) in Roanoke, Virginia. The show followed the man, a chiropractor by profession, as he went about his daily life before treatment and after he'd gone to Hollins for an immersive, intensive three-week program. Following completion of the program, his ability to speak fluently—for the first time in his life— was simply astonishing.

That was all it took for me.

I couldn't take a three week leave of absence, but in March 1977, I signed up for a course that took place over thirteen weekends at a university in upstate New York.

During my three months in the program, I received exctly the intensive therapy I'd hoped for. I learned new ways to use my speech muscles to control my stuttering and to speak fluently at will.

Fluency starts with a slow, comfortable, full breath. There are several different techniques, as well as techniques for different sounds you are taught to focus on. There's I, U, and on down the list. One technique is full breath and amplitude contour. Amplitude contour is when you start speaking with a softness to the word, and then you go up, and then you go down again. There are several targets—how to pronounce hard consonants, the Ks, Ts, and Cs. Stutterers tend to speak on exhaled breath. Fluent speakers are always speaking on a comfortable full breath, and that's one of the things stutterers learn at Hollins.

I gave it my all in the program and HCRI stuttering therapy changed my life. I finally felt I had fluency targets to hold onto, and if I practiced them religiously, I could be fluent most of the time, and in some cases, all the time.

When I returned home, I regularly practiced the skills I'd learned in order to habituate my newly acquired fluency. More than 60% of Hollins attendees go back for a refresher course. I did the same in April 1993. I also attended the annual three-day workshops every July for fifteen years. Astronaut and Senator John Glenn's lovely wife, Annie, who was also a stutterer, attended with me. We became good friends.

I was so grateful for my profound and prolonged improvement that a friend and I set up a scholarship. Each year, we send three young people to HCRI tuition free. I keep up with many of the scholarship recipients, and all have benefitted from this terrific program.

ROADBLOCK

WITH MY STUTTERING UNDER EXCELLENT CONTROL,
I was able to excel in my role as Director of Marketing at Lederle Laboratories. I continued to work harder and smarter and even became known for making sure I tried whatever vaccine or medicine whose campaign I was heading up—pill, injection, or otherwise. It was important to me to know how each drug felt and understand any side effects. I was responsible for marketing two products that were developed for the Central Nervous System: Loxitane, and an antidepressant called Amoxapine.

I tried both.

I felt that having this information better enabled me to guide the drug representatives who presented our products to highly respected, well-known MDs. Medical education was everything in those days, and I wanted the doctors to have as much information as possible in order to prescribe our drug to their patients.

I oversaw vaccines, drugs, and generics. I had the number one group in the company, and our pneumonia and influenza vaccines were number one worldwide. Although I was running the company's most successful divisions, I began to notice that people below me and colleagues with much less in the way of accomplishment were regularly moving past me, and I had no idea why.

Eventually, the job of General Manager opened up. Because I was the guy coming up with the most innovative ideas, and could sell them to my boss and then watch the drugs succeed in the general public, I was a shoe-in for the promotion.

Instead, they gave it to a manufacturing guy.

I was frustrated, hurt, depressed, and angry. After running into brick walls with my boss and human resources and not being able to get any kind of a straight answer as to why I wasn't moved up to General Manager, I took a call from an executive recruiter. The opportunity was a small advertising agency whose owner offered me a twenty percent equity spot.

It was 1983 when I took the job and left Lederle, the company I had cherished for eighteen years.

WE SHOULD TALK

I WANTED MY MARRIAGE TO BE BETTER THAN MY parents' had been. It was a fairly low bar, but from the beginning, my marriage was not ideal. We had our good moments. We did manage to create two wonderful children—Pamela who was born in 1966 and Jonathon who came along in 1969.

We became closer being parents, loved our kids tremendously, and went on some great family vacations, the highlight of which was a trip I won as a bonus to Disneyworld.

Much like my own father, my life was focused on work and career, but when I came home in the evening, I did as much as I could to be with my kids. In retrospect, I believe it was a mistake to think of work as number one—particularly where my kids were concerned. There should have been more balance, but we both had defined roles: me as the breadwinner and Susan as the homemaker.

Unfortunately, my wife's parents meddled in our relationship, felt free to interfere with my career goals, and let themselves into the house whenever they felt like coming over. My wife didn't see that as a problem, but I definitely did.

In the meantime, I didn't want the children to suffer the emotional and psychological stress of a divorce, so I remained married for twenty not terribly happy years.

I'd like to say I was heartbroken when she went to her high school reunion, met up with her old boyfriend, and they reignited their relationship. We went to counseling to try and work things out, but the counselor pulled me aside afterwards and told me it was hopeless—my wife was in love with someone else. In the end, and after an inevitable difficult transition period, it was something of a relief to grant her a divorce. In fact, when things went awry financially for her and her new husband (which happened more than once), I gave them money to bail them out.

KLEMPTNER / SAATCHI & SAATCHI

AFTER BEING PASSED OVER FOR PROMOTION AT the small Glassman Agency in New Jersey, I decided to move on into the bigger advertising world in New York. I went over to the Saatchi and Saatchi group as senior vice president of its healthcare operations. I was there for two years, and it turned out to be a boring tenue.

Looking back, I believe this is when I began to see that as an employee or a vendor, my first obligation was to my employer and client, and they deserved nothing but my best. I later went on to formulate these thoughts as a value statement for the Becker Euro R.S.C.G. agency, where I would soon take the reins.

MECHELE, MY BELLE

SEEING AS MY MARRIAGE HAD FALLEN APART WHILE
I was at Lederle, and my future was headed in an entirely new direction, my plan was to date but never marry again.

One of my fraternity brothers from Ohio State happened to live out in the Hamptons. He was a nice guy, who I helped out back at school when people tried to make fun of him for being gay. We'd become lifelong friends. A friend of his named Faith Popcorn told him, "You have to fix my sister up."

"The only guy I know got divorced less than a year ago, so I'm not fixing you up with him," he told her.

Faith was persuasive, and Michael agreed to throw a cocktail party at his apartment in Manhattan. The only straight people invited were me and Faith's attractive sister, Mechele, who was a petite brunette spitfire with pretty brown eyes and the best smile I've ever seen.

After the cocktail party, Michael took us out for dinner. It was a lovely evening filled with interesting conversation and plenty of laughter.

Afterwards, I gave Mechele a lift home—nothing more. Mechele was attractive, very nice, smart, and thirteen years my junior, but, as Michael assumed, I wasn't interested in getting entangled with anyone, ever again.

A couple weeks later, I was in the car driving home from work, and there was Mechele on the street hailing a cab.

I stopped and gave her a lift home.

She invited me up for a cup of coffee.

As it turned out, Mechele was not only attractive and charming, but impossibly accomplished. Also, a native of New York City, she'd earned a B.A. cum laude from American University in Washington, D.C., an M.A. in American folklore from the University of Pennsylvania, followed by an M.B.A. at Columbia University. She'd worked at Seagram and Sons as a brand manager and at the Thompson Medical Company as the brand director for Slim-Fast.

We started to date.

After a few dates around the city I said, "What are you doing this summer?"

"I'm going to Nice, France, to the university, to work on my French," she said.

"I've never been to Nice. Do you mind if I come for a weekend?" I asked her.

"Sure," she said.

Mechele met me at the airport looking lovely and stylish. We went to a great hotel, and she arranged a trolley trip around Nice. It was romantic, beautiful, and we fell in love on that trip.

Shortly thereafter, I moved into her co-op in the East Village.

When Mechele wanted to get married, I wasn't quite ready, but we found a place on 38th on the Upper East Side, and we stayed there for a couple years. By then, my daughter Pamela was getting married.

"You have a wonderful relationship with Mechele," she said. "You should get married as well."

I gave it a lot of thought…

On March 25, 1990, I married Mechele—the love of my life and the greatest asset I could ever imagine. We bought our place at 630 Park Avenue as a married couple and began our happily ever after.

Mechele was an incredible asset and successful in her own right. She began working for her sister, Faith Popcorn, becoming the president of BrainReserve a "future-focused consultancy serving the Fortune 500." She formed her own trend-analysis company, Marketing Fire, and spoke nationally and internationally about consumer trends. She also found time to run her family's real estate company, Fame, a combination of the first two letters of her and her sister's names.

My wife had a unique ability to think through an issue and come up with several different conclusions to fix the problem. When I was being recruited by Becker, they offered me more money than I was making, but Mechele said, "Sander, go back to them, take a reduction in your salary, and come up with a performance incentive deal. Let them know that for everything over three million in profit you make you will get one-third."

"Mechele, the company is losing money."

"I know you. You will make them money," she said.

The people at Becker were thrilled by my proposition. They were even more thrilled when I led the global company to number two in the world. With a third of the profits over three million, I was also thrilled! I was promoted to global CEO after I took the U.S. Division from the red into the black after the first two years.

I quickly grew to rely on Mechele's business savvy and involved her in everything from important decisions to having her by my side for client dinners. Everyone was utterly charmed by her intelligence, warmth, and upbeat personality. Mechele never said negative things about others.

We traveled the world together, visiting a different place every year. I believe the only places we didn't get to were India and Japan. We jogged together every day from 66th to 88th streets, and I put a plaque on a park bench in Central Park in honor of her on August 8, 2007. Mechele's pet name for me was "Growlie." My pet name for her was "Foxy."

The bench says: *For the world's best person. My wife and biggest supporter. Thanks, Foxy…From Growlie.*

She made me happy and did good things for me she knew I liked. She was wonderful with my kids and her family, particularly her Uncle Sugar added to her positive influence.

My friend and former co-worker Deb Stevens tells me that everyone at work knew that if things went poorly at the office on any given day, I would show up at work much better the next, and they always attributed my improved mood to Mechele's calming, grounding influence.

Deb reminded me of a dinner we had with her one evening. She and her partner, Peter, were talking about buying an apartment. Conversative, Deb wanted to make sure they bought something they could really afford. Mechele said, "You have to reach. Don't be afraid to reach."

To this day, whenever she is making a financial decision, Peter will tell her, "But Mechele would say you have to reach."

BECKER

IN 1988, I WAS RECRUITED TO TAKE CHARGE OF A SMALL
advertising agency called Robert A Becker, Euro R.S.C.G. (now
Havas Health), whose clients were all in the pharmaceutical industry.
I suppose you could say, there my adventures began.

I arrived for my first day of work on August 8, 1988 at 8:15
AM. The elevator didn't work, so I had to take the staircase. When
I got up to the ninth floor, a little sweatier than I would have pre-
ferred, the door to the office was locked. I had to wait for someone
to arrive. I was already unnerved when I stepped into my office
and discovered that it needed some servicing. Much to her cha-
grin, I instructed Terry Wachalter the longtime office manager, the
wall outlets were crooked and needed to be fixed.

It was the beginning of a longtime friendship and business part-
nership, but I know for a fact that her first impression of me was a
lot more along the lines of "Oh, I am in for a rocky ride."

Those little glitches were harbingers of much bigger issues. At
the time I was recruited, I was not made aware that the firm's
primary clients, Merck and Sandoz, had decided to reassign their
business elsewhere. The future of the agency was also in jeopardy

as the original owners, WCRS, had lost confidence in their invest-ment and sold it to Euro RSCG. The English at that time owned the Becker agency. and the recruiter went over the owner, Bob Becker's head, as well as the president, Joel Lauber, to bring me in. They did not make my life easy.

Bob Becker was well into retirement age when I came on board. We didn't have the greatest relationship, possibly because we were more alike than we cared to admit.

"When are you going to leave, Bob? You're already 80 years old?"

"Not me," he said. "As a matter of fact, when we move offices, I want an office again with my own bathroom."

"No way," I said. "You're not getting your own bathroom. If I have to go to the public men's room, you have to go to the public men's room."

On the day Bob Becker finally retired, the English owners moved me into a position above Joel Lauber, so he now reported to me. Needless to say, he wasn't thrilled.

I had a lot of work ahead of me to straighten out the company.

HONG LUCK

I SETTLED INTO MY NEW ROLE, AND THEN, LATER
that year, on a snowy Christmas Eve, I got a call from a former
senior vice president for Lederle named George Bywater.

"Sander, I need to meet you for lunch up in Pearl River," he
said.

"George, it's snowing like crazy, and it's Christmas Eve," I said.

"Sander, I resigned my position. I have prostate cancer, and I
probably have another six months to live. I need to see you."

The visibility was zero as I crossed the Tappan Zee (now Mario
Cuomo) bridge, headed upstate, and met George at a well-known
restaurant called Hong Luck, famous for power lunches. A strong
martini awaited my arrival.

"Sander, enjoy your martini, and then I'll tell you why I needed
to see you," George said.

I'm not a drinker, and I had a treacherous drive back, so I picked
up the glass and took a small sip for show.

"Listen," he finally said. "You need to know there's a member
of our board who said we couldn't give a big job at the company
to Sander because stuttering is a manifestation of mental illness."

I was both stunned and furious. I could clearly see the "glass ceiling" I had faced. I'd performed at the top level for years, but I hadn't anticipated that my stuttering could possibly become an insurmountable impediment — certainly not because of one influential superior's ignorance. It was truly horrifying at a company devoted to science and knowledge. As I drove back in that snowstorm, I vowed to do whatever it took to be more successful than any of the people I'd worked with at Lederle by never again being blinded to the realities of any situation.

OUT OF THE RED

ALONG WITH MY TEAM, I REBUILT BECKER FROM scratch. To do so, it was necessary to cut the staff from seventy to forty people. I then recruited former clients who understood it wasn't about just winning creative awards but jumping the revenue curve for their products. Some of the people I hired made more money than me, but I didn't care. By the same token, if I met a person with the right customer service skills, the right interpersonal skills and worked hard—whether working as a trainer at my health club or waiting on me at a restaurant— I would recruit them to Becker and have HR figure out what to do with them. In my mind, Becker was a blue-collar agency, meaning we worked hard and never rested on our laurels.

Our mission statement was, *If it ain't great we don't do it or show it. We exist to sell our clients' products.* Our strategy could be boiled down to one word: innovation. We were always looking for the Big Idea, never knowing where it would come from.

When we won the Flomax account (Flomax treats benign prostatic hypertrophy), we were facing two competitors with slightly better data and significantly larger ad budgets. I think our client would have been satisfied with meeting its sales quota and a respectable third place market share. Our creative team came up with an idea that was unheard of at the time. We created a commercial showing a family touring the country with a porta potty hitched to the back of the car. This not only dramatized the problem of never having to stop to urinate, but it also wiped out any stigma for taking the medication. Almost overnight, we made Flomax the number one BPH product globally.

When we lost a new business pitch, I would tell the team they could take the afternoon to feel bad about losing, but *tomorrow we're going to come back stronger, we're going to go after the competitive brand, we're going to use everything we learned to show it to somebody else who's going to appreciate what we do.*

In two years, I took Becker out of the red and was made global president. By 1998, the company employed over 220 people. I'd met Merck's Senior Vice President, Shelly Berkle, at a pharmaceutical manufacturer's convention, and we hit it off, so he sent over business. I'd also done work with Rick Lane at Merck, and I got a lot of business from him.

It's a challenge to get so many people moving in the same direction and all with the same mission; that is crucial yet lacking in many companies today. I think I was able to achieve that because of my firm belief that what we were doing was so important and that we were all going to achieve it together. As a person who was really focused on new and better ways of jumping the revenue curve, I was interested in having present clients give us more business because we made them look good. We had notable people like

Al Paz, Terry Gallo, and Terry Wachalter. They did a heck of a job with our clients.

Over the next decade, we introduced six blockbuster two billion dollar healthcare brands, as well as a number of brands with smaller sales that often had a big impact on patient's lives.

Having gained many of the country's premiere pharmaceutical companies as clients, including Aventis, Bayer, Boehringer-Ingelheim, Bristol-Myers Squibb, Glaxo SmithKline, Merck, Rhone-Poulenc Rorer [now Sanofi] Roche, and Wyeth and launching or restaging brands, such as Cefzil, Effexor, Flomax, Flonase, Flovent, Mobic, Plavix, and Zosyn as well as numerous specialty brands in therapeutic categories such as oncology [Xeloda], [Revlimid] organ transplant [Rapamune] and emergency medicine [Retavase], Euro RSCG Becker (now Havas) became the world's second-largest healthcare marketing firm.

In 2000, we introduced Zerit, a major HIV product for Bristol Myers Squibb. My team and I departed from the standard focus on professional medical journals and ran ads directed to the gay communities—in their neighborhoods, in subways, buses, etc. Zerit became an essential component in the triple-therapy that finally helped make HIV a manageable disease.

Going directly to the public was unconventional at the time, but HIV was a unique challenge. Many patients knew more about their disease than the average internist. It's worth noting that we were soon copied by just about everyone.

During those years, my speech and disfluencies improved dramatically, but the stuttering didn't go away. I was CEO of a publicly traded company, and still, I'd get locked up on a word and freeze in a room full of people. Stuttering is like a deluge that finds you when you least expect it. You have to just come back to your breath and start again. Gather the little sticks first, and be patient as you regain the ground.

Telephone will always be the most difficult. Stutterers call the telephone the devil's instrument because you tend to focus more on the phone than you do one on one. You're not looking at the person. You don't see the smile on the other person's face. It's you and this thing in your hand. The biggest challenge I ever had was pitching a client by phone. In my talks to stutterers, I spoke about the importance of speech practice on the phone. I still do.

In running a big agency, I had to pitch against competitive agencies and that was a challenge. Sometimes, I'd be standing outside of the conference room listening to my competitor, who was there before me do their pitches and think, "Wow, terrific idea!" or "So articulate!" Then, of course, I had to come in, introduce my team, and give a short bio on each of them. I had to be great. We had to win the business, and I couldn't block or stammer my head off.

I never did a presentation unless I rehearsed, rehearsed, rehearsed. Of course, I took a beta-blocker drug, as well. I remembered to focus not so much on what I was saying but how I would say it.

To make sure I was always at my best, I got up and went to the gym at five in the morning every day. I would run five miles on the treadmill, shower, and be the first one into work in the morning. At night, I went out to dinner with clients or prospective clients three or four nights a week. I was totally dedicated to building the business and being in the best physical shape to take on whatever challenge came my way.

People with disabilities often find they have to contribute more and make a bigger impact on the firm than their contemporaries. I never let stuttering or anything else get in the way of moving my division of RSCG Becker forward.

MAD MENSCH

THERE WERE A LOT OF CHALLENGES, AND I HAVE NO doubt Becker was a difficult place to work at times. We definitely had high turnover. I was very specific about the things I wanted and what was needed. I'm definitely the guy who has all the pencils pointed in the same direction in my desk drawer, and I expect precision—from prompt attendance at meetings to the corporate dress code. I was always in a suit, complete with a crisply starched and monogrammed shirt. Jeans, even on casual Fridays, were a non-starter! I sent more than one young man home for lack of a collared shirt, and women who showed up in a dress more suited for a Saturday night than the office got the same treatment. People sometimes worked until midnight or even later, and they certainly didn't relish being confronted by their CEO when they came in late the next morning, but I held them to the same standards I maintained for myself.

When we did pitches for new business, I would go through the decks my people put expected together multiple times and change words individually. It had to be perfect. I lived by two mottos: *If it aint great don't do it* and *If it ain't great don't show it*. I had no problem telling a client something wasn't ready yet and that we needed a few more days.

As a result, my core group of people are dispersed throughout the industry, many of them leading agencies on their own.

I remember one time we had won so much new business and we really needed to catch up in terms of staffing. My team was overwhelmed with trying to fill those positions. Deb Stevens, our HR manager said, "Sander, we can't pitch any more new business until we make some progress catching up."

"Don't ever say that to me again," I said. I meant it. As soon as you walked into reception there was a big sign that said, *Growth is Survival.* I really believed that if you weren't growing you weren't going to survive. We had to figure out how to accommodate the business, and we did.

Some of my best memories from my days at Becker include Veteran's Day, where I gave anyone who had served in the military the day off, and I invited all those who didn't take the day to join me for a walk over to Fifth Avenue, where we watched the parade. I looked forward to it every year. Another memorable night was December 31, 1999. Y2K was upon us, so I decided to throw a big New Year's Eve bash for the employees and their families. We went all out—black-tie, gourmet catering, and great music. We invited my friend, the then New York City police commissioner, Howard Safir, and his wife, Carol. The police officers in the lobby had no idea he was coming, so when he and Carol arrived, they treated him like a movie star at a red-carpet event. Some of the cops had never met their popular police commissioner before, and they reveled in the opportunity to shake his hand and chat with him. The party was great fun. Our company was on a high floor at 1633 Broadway, and we could see the ball drop at midnight from the giant picture windows facing the tower. We rang 2000 in high style.

The Becker years were memorable—in ways both good and challenging—for many reasons. They left strong impressions on most everyone who worked with us. I developed many of my closest friendships and most enduring bonds during that time period. I asked some of those employees turned lifelong friends to fill in with impressions and memories they had of their job, their interactions with me, and anything else they wanted to contribute about our time working together—and beyond.

MARK GOLDSTONE (INVESTOR):

I FIRST MET SANDER IN LONDON IN 1991 AFTER WE had both been acquired by the French group which ultimately became Havas. We talked a lot about the healthcare space and built a connection straightaway,y which ultimately led to Sander bringing me over to the U. S. offices.

I learned fairly quickly to give Sander an advance heads-up about whoever was going to be in any meetings we had together. If I went in and said, "Okay, Sander, here's what's happening. The guy on the left is going to be the such and such... he's this... don't mention this to him. The guy in the middle, he's the one we want to talk to. Say this to him."

When I did, Sander was phenomenal. He'd knock it out of the park.

One day, Sander appeared in my office.

"Mark, you're coming with me," he said.

"Where are we going?" I asked.

"Dan Vasella is in town. He's making a speech down at the Harvard Club."

This was at about 5:00 in the afternoon, and we went down to the Harvard Club. Sander, of course, sat in the front row.

Dan Vasella, who was CEO of Novartis, gave a great speech about healthcare. Within a nanosecond of him finishing the speech, Sander was up at the podium beside him with his hand out. "Dan Vasella, Sander Flaum, great to meet you."

Dan looked sort of taken aback by this. "Sander Flaum...?"

"Yes, Sander. The bagels. The H&H bagels."

As it turned out, Sander was relentless and would send H&H bagels to Dan Vasella in Switzerland every month.

"You're the bagel guy?" Dan Vasella asked, making the connection and smiling.

It was a brilliant long play on Sander's part.

DOREEN ECKERT (EXECUTIVE VICE PRESIDENT, PARTNER, EVOKE)

I INTERVIEW A LOT OF JUNIOR PEOPLE, AND I GO TO hiring fairs, and potential candidates will ask me, "How did you get started in the industry?"

I always answer, "Not the way you're getting started!"

I met Sander in 1999 on Christmas Eve at Robert's Restaurant in Water Mill, N.Y. I waited on him and Mechele at the restaurant. I was an art history major looking at graduate schools, painting, waiting tables, and searching for apartments in New York. Sander grilled me on the menu because he was on the Atkins diet and wanted to make sure there was no sugar in anything he was eating. He loved that I knew how everything was prepared.

At the end of the meal, he asked, "What do you do?"

"It's Christmas Eve, and I'm waiting on you. This is what I do."

"Have you ever thought about healthcare advertising?" he asked.

"That would be like working for the devil." I definitely had a very different opinion!

"What are you talking about? We help people. You should come in," he said, writing his information on the back of the restaurant's card.

I talked to some people and realized he was the CEO, so I put a résumé together

and went into Becker the next week.

I met Lisa and Deb who asked, "How fast do you type?"

"Oh, I don't type," I said.

"Recreate this PowerPoint slide," they said,

"I don't even know what PowerPoint is."

They both had to think Sander was crazy, but luckily, we had good chemistry.

"There's something in you," Sander said. "Where do you want to go in the agency, sweetheart? You're creative, you can go anywhere."

He sent me for Excel classes, and I was mentored by one of the creative directors in PowerPoint slide design and storytelling. As a result, I realized that I really loved the front of the room and presenting and the strategy aspects. Sander gave me an opportunity on the account services side, and I have been doing that ever since, but I started out as a second assistant to Sander.

I quickly decided my job there was just like waiting tables. I needed to keep Sander happy and to anticipate what he needed. If I did that, I would do fine. I learned to be there early because Sander would call the phone to make sure you were in your seat ready to go. If it was 8:05, he would basically respond to the good morning with good afternoon because you were late. At 8:10, the yogurt had to be set out with the spoon a certain way, and the coffee had to be there, magazines were fanned, and emails were highlighted and laid out for him because he didn't actually like going on the computer so much then. He would come in with dictation tapes from his ride for me to type up. He would

74

have whatever he'd read from The Wall Street Journal, *etc., for me to make copies of and distribute to whomever he felt needed to see them. Sander was particular but very consistent in his expectations of what good looked like and wanted everyone to live up to their full potential.*

If, for example, Sander went to China and bought gifts for clients, I would deal with customs to get the pottery through into the country on time. There was a gift closet containing pens, cufflinks etc., and a gift database for all of the clients with addresses, birthdays, anniversaries and names of spouses and children. We organized for him to bring flowers to receptionists and recent articles of interest to fellow CEOs. It was very old school, and I have yet to see an executive office who does it since, but we knew what the latest Hermes tie or scarf was and which ones we'd given, and to whom, so we didn't send a repeat gift.

Because I worked in the C-suite, I also got to see the human sides of Sander— when he was stressed about a family member or worried about someone in the office. I have never worked for a CEO in any company that truly cared as much about others.

DEB STEVENS, PRESIDENT, DEB STEVENS CONSULTING:

SANDER DEFINITELY HAD AN EYE FOR FINDING talented people. Anyone he thought had potential made their way in for an interview. His personal trainer, Rachel, became an art director and, eventually, a creative director in the industry. Another gentleman, James, was a grad student in London. We had to figure out the immigration process, but he turned out to be brilliant. We drew the line when he wanted to bring in the locker room attendant from his gym because he didn't speak English well enough to find a position for him.

At one point, Sander insisted we hire a difficult, quirky individual and made him head of one of our divisions (a division that didn't yet exist) because Sander knew the man was a money maker and was going to do right by the business. It was our job to figure out how to get along him!

As exacting as he was, Sander cared about his people both professionally and personally. He didn't like when people were single and tried to set them up. He offered new wardrobes. If he didn't like someone's haircut, he sent them to his barber. He even offered to pay for braces or new teeth. And when somebody resigned, especially someone he was close to, he took it really hard.

The people who got along best with Sander learned to appreciate or overlook his quirks. For instance, he would pat me on the head. I didn't care because I knew it came from a place of kindness. People who took exception and let that really dictate their experience didn't last long.

When we grew to 350 people and were combined with the other companies, I was truly impressed by how he was able to get everyone to move in the same direction. People would say after interviews they were surprised that no matter who they met during the interview process, everybody said the same thing about the agency and knew what we were doing. Sander was the leader at the top who made sure we knew why we were there every day, what we were supposed to be about, and what we stood for.

GUY DESS (CO-FOUNDER, BULLSEYE HEALTHCARE):

WHEN I WAS INTERVIEWING, SANDER TOLD ME THERE really wasn't a head of Creative and that I could have that job if everything worked out.

It did.

We were getting pretty big back then. We had Bristol Myers Squibb and Lederle as clients and a lot of business as a result. There was always a lot going on. We would get to the point of having a campaign done or a major ad being done and were all in agreement that it was good. Sander didn't like to see everybody in his office at the same time, so I would go in and we'd sit down, and we'd go over it. I'd show him the concept and the various iterations and details. 99% of the time he say, "Guy, what is this crap? This is terrible. This is what you bring me? I can't believe that you, of all the people I trust, bring me this stuff. Do you really like this? It's horrible!"

Sander would then go through every inch of it while I'd sit there, and I'd take notes.

Afterwards, I'd regroup with the team and say, "Okay, this is what we have to do."

Everyone would be like, "What? How is that possible?"

It took me some back and forth, and about two years, to figure out that this is what had to happen and we'd change everything to what he wanted: we'd rewrite this, move that, change this color, move that sideways. Whatever he asked for, I had the team do.

When I'd go back into Sander, he'd say, "This is brilliant. This is fantastic. This is what I'm talking about. You did a great job. The team is great, you saw this through, you delivered exactly what I wanted, it's perfect, I love it. We're going to take it to the client tomorrow."

He wouldn't say, "You did it my way" but that I'd done it and the team did it.

Then I'd come back out, and everyone would be all nervous, and I'd say, "It's good, we're all good."

LISA POLLIONE (CHIEF OF STAFF)

I BEGAN AS A TEMP AT BECKER IN THE '90'S. WE WERE
located at 1633 Broadway at the time. One day, I was picking up
mail and messages for my direct report at the reception desk. I began
chatting with a nice man standing there. He introduced himself as
Sander, and I introduced myself as well. He asked me my name and
who I worked for. He then told me that he and his wife had just come
back from South Africa and that it was their first trip to that country.
We chatted a bit more about his trip, and we ended our conversation.

I had no idea he was the CEO of the company.

As a temp, I floated to a couple of different areas within the com-
pany. One day, I received a call asking me to come into the CEO's
office to interview as his assistant. I followed directions as to where
the office was, walked in, and there was Sander, the man I met at the
reception desk days earlier! I couldn't believe I had been talking with
the CEO and had no idea.

Little did I know, he had specifically asked for me when a position
came up working as his assistant. I had never worked for a C-suite
executive, so I was nervous because this was so new to me, but I was
flattered they thought of me for the position.

I learned soon after that the last seven executive assistants had come and gone in short order. One even went to lunch and never came back. I took a deep breath and dove on into the job.

Things were stressful for the first couple of months. I was terribly busy every day with whatever projects needed to be completed and making client appointments for Sander. Sander had to have a daily agenda card with him each day along with the coordinated client folders for the respective meetings. On the card was the client's name, mobile, assistant's name, her mobile, plus wife's name, kids, new baby, and when Sander first met the client, if he didn't know them already. I also would remind him to "see file" that was in his bag set up for the meeting. In the file would be notes from when they last met, plus any new articles I would research prior to the meeting.

I also started making lists of things to do, and Sander ended up loving them so much he had writing pads made up called "Things To Do" at the top of the page followed by twelve lines underneath.

I'd go into his office each morning to discuss what had to get done. I would return to my desk to get underway, and I would hear my name repeatedly.

I would go back into his office, and he would add an item to the new daily list.

Two seconds after I got back to my desk, I would be called in to add another item to the list. And again…

This went on almost every day, several times a day to the point where after he called out my name yet again, I broke down and shouted, "Oh what?"

Sander looked up, smiled, and said, "I'm sorry, Sweetheart. Is there a problem?"

"Sir," I said, "This back and forth is killing me, I am exhausted, and the day just started! Can we rethink the calling me back and forth all morning, to where you just make a list or leave me a message of things you want done?" We worked it out eventually, and then we hit our stride together.

My assistant at the time said, "There are people stopping and listening to the banter, including me, between the two of you like it's a tennis match or a comedy." I guess there were some funny moments between us at 1633 Broadway.

Sander was a very passionate CEO. He cared deeply about how the day's events would go with a client. And if something one of his direct reports said or did something to upset him, he would sometimes go off the rails and start yelling. During those times, there were immediate meetings with Deb Stevens and Terry Wachalter in Sander's office, where they would shut his door and calm him down. All of the sudden, you'd hear one of the ladies say, "Sander, you can't do this" or "you cannot say that." Some of the other employees would hear the shouting coming from the "wall people" (those who had an office on the wall) and were wondering if there was dissention in the ranks. Then there was silence, sometimes even an apology, and we all moved on. As for me, I always had a bag of Hershey's chocolates on the bottom right drawer of my desk (thanks to Carol's instruction) so the moment one of these events happened, I got the bag out of the drawer and left his favorites on the desk. He'd put the wrappers in the garbage after that and say, "Thanks, sweetheart."

At the end of most days, he met clients after work and didn't want his briefcase with him, so he had me send home "the bag." I often had to hire a cab and let Frank the doorman know it was on its way and to be outside awaiting its arrival. At one point, I started going back to college at night to finish my degree at Hunter College, so I would drop the bag off on my way to class.

The next morning, we started all over again.

TERRY WACHALTER
(CHIEF OPERATING OFFICER):

I MET SANDER FOR THE FIRST TIME ON AUGUST 8, 1988.
He greeted me by telling me that there was a duplex receptacle on his
wall that was crooked and to get it fixed.

I knew I was in for it!

The unique thing I soon discovered about Sander was that, on one
hand, he was tyrannical and a tough cookie. On the other hand, he
was warm and fuzzy.

Although I was the office manager at Becker, I was also a finance
person. Because he trusted me and didn't feel like he could talk to the
people who were in the position, he had me working as a go-between,
and I would feed to him everything he needed to run the business the
way he wanted to and to make it more successful. That culminated in
my becoming chief financial officer.

I dealt with the demanding side of Sander—from enforcing his
dress code for Dress Down Fridays (no jeans, collared shirts, appropri-
ate dresses, and, heaven forbid, no tennis shoes) to the voicemail system
(I had check it at least ten times a day because inevitably there was
always a message from Sander in the middle of the night on Saturday,

Sunday morning, anytime day or night). I even went to the diction classes he signed me up for because he felt it was important that I lose my Bronx accent. While other people would have been taken aback, I knew he was just doing for me what he would want done for him.

I saw the very warm side of him, especially when we started doing things with his trusts, and finally, we formed a foundation, which enabled him to give and continue to support over fifty charities. He was always so pro-woman and was the first one to support anyone who had the appropriate intelligence to assist and getting them where he felt they should be.

I certainly benefitted from his advocacy and from our terrific friendship of over forty years.

DOUBLE TALK

DURING MY TENURE, ROBERT A. BECKER WAS BOUGHT by a company called Euro RSCG, which was British based and became Robert A. Becker Euro RSCG. After that, it was bought by a French company, Havas Health Advertising. During the time it was transitioning to the French company, we quickly lost several financial people.

I began to ask Terry Wachalter to step in and accomplish some of the things I needed that couldn't be handled with the financial folks now in charge. My trust and dependence on her resulted in her moving from office manager to Chief Financial Officer. It was something of a task given our French management who didn't believe in having women in such high positions. I, however, have always believed in promoting and supporting anyone who has shown themselves capable.

In 1995, Robert A. Becker was listed as runner-up for Agency of the Year by *Medical Advertising News.* In 2003, Robert A. Becker was named Agency of the Year by *Medical Advertising News,* and I was named 2003's Man of the Year.

At the time, the agency's net revenue was $60 million annually and had seven of the top 10 pharmaceutical companies as clients.

While serving as Chief Executive Officer of Euro RSCG Worthwide, Bob S. took over the responsibility of healthcare marketing companies, Robert A. Becker and Lally McFarland Pantello, which were rolled into the Euro RSCG group.

At that time, I was CEO of Robert A. Becker Euro RSCG, and Ron Pantello was CEO of Lally McFarland Pantello EURO RSCG.

Since there were now two individuals running two healthcare networks, consolidation was inevitable. Both Ron Pantello and I were asked separately by Mr. S. to put together a 5-year plan to run the total healthcare group. After presenting the plan, Mr. S decided to make Ron Pantello the head of the group and merged us all together. It was supposed to be a fair comparison, but Mr. S. never showed me or our group any respect for our accomplishments. It was a foregone conclusion that Pantello would "win."

There was no place for me in the mix, so at the end of my contract in December 2003, I left Robert A. Becker EURO RSCG.

My parting gift from the whole company was a pair of autographed jeans laid out in a shadow box, and everybody signed the jeans.

As I joked to Terry, "Of all the employee programs I started at Becker to help my employees advance and grow in their careers, I will be most remembered for my stance on wearing jeans in the office!

PART III
TALKING THE TALK

FLAUM PARTNERS /
FLAUM NAVIGATORS

IN 2004, I STARTED MY OWN COMPANY, Flaum Partners Inc., in beautiful new offices at 420 Lexington in New York City.

As a result of non-compete agreements, I wasn't allowed to take clients or employees with me, nor approach any of them for a specified period of time. Many clients came over to our firm later. The same went for employees like Terry Wachalter, who quit Havas after suffering insufferable insults and false accusations. She called from a phone booth to tell me her harrowing story.

"You stay right there. I'm coming to meet you," I said.

I made her my head of operations on the spot.

Together, we did a lot of cold calling, mailings, and made personal phone calls. It took at least two months to get the company moving. We landed some small business, which turned out well for the client and led to additional business. We soon brought in Bristol Meyers Squibb via Don Hayden in Evansville, Indiana.

Deb Stevens, who ran human resources for Becker, and eventually left there herself, helped recruit staff as I started to grow the new company.

When Deb told me she was leaving to start her own company, I handed her the paperweight that had been on my desk for years. It said, "If you're not the lead dog, the view never changes."

I'd already learned that lesson myself.

Lisa Pollione, my assistant of twenty years stayed with me—thank goodness.

My wife, Mechele, was always there to support me and address any concerns I had, over who I met, how I met them, or how I would best serve them.

I'd learned a lot from my years at Becker and Lederle and cared deeply for my teams there and the clients I worked for. As I'd done for years, I continued to make it a point to call someone if they lost their job, something happened to them, or I heard they were passed over for a promotion. I didn't assume people knew I was there. I always reached out to find out what was going on.

Flaum Partners took off quickly. Our mission—to help companies in the pharmaceutical industry accelerate their business growth through transformational ideas that galvanized leadership, brand building, and innovation—resonated across the industry. It helped that we employed the best people, few of whom were from advertising, but former clients and industry standouts. As a result, we had better, more innovative products and ideas than our competitors.

Together, we developed the first persistency program, the first patient guarantee program, the first indigent patient program, the first adherence program, and the first "War Games" program. Because we insisted on challenging conventional wisdom, we were able to assist clients in confronting daunting odds and reinventing themselves to maintain their market advantage.

Initially, we limited our services to consulting, but clients soon requested that we take over advertising responsibilities, and we grew to over fifty employees.

There were many successes but also noteworthy mistakes. One of my biggest was to hire a head of operations who also served as something of a co-president. It was to be a horrible move. Despite a record of client interaction, she could not bring in new business, and the people she hired were awful. She began to drive our business into the ground. She realized pretty quickly that she was never going to make it and stopped trying. She resigned the day I was going to let her go, but I waited too long. The damage had been done. I'd learned a painful lesson about checking references, not just via the résumé, but by calling former bosses to see what they really thought of their former employees.

We were in business until the end of 2010 when Terry Wachalter retired. I was not ready to retire yet. I had so much more I wanted to do. I then formed Flaum Navigators, Inc., a pharmaceutical marketing, leadership, and communication consultancy, which is still in business today.

PAYING IT FORWARD

IN MY MANY YEARS OF CONSULTING AND MENTORING, I identified common threads in behavior among those who have suffered career setbacks by examining how they coped with those setbacks, how they rebounded from them, and how they turned a loss into a gain, thus creating an opportunity to rejuvenate their professional and personal lives.

Because I went through a few major professional setbacks in my own life, I was able to see how these same threads ran through my own experience. Like these other professionals, I went into an emotional tailspin fueled by unhealthy, unproductive feelings that I gradually—and with difficulty and some good mentors—pulled myself out of, regaining a sense of clarity and purpose.

Focusing on my strengths and not on the feeling that the whole world was out to get me, I was able to turn various corners in my own professional life. I made it a point to become a mentor to many other stutterers. I told them to let people know at the outset that they stutter. It clears the air and dissipates that cringey moment when you block on a word.

It's a lot easier at this stage of my life to talk about the speech impediment and some of the things that I did to overcome the tension and fear of speaking. When you're comfortable enough with yourself to say, "I happen to be a stutterer," it goes a long way to make your speech impediment a non-issue.

Mentoring has become something you do at the end of a career. I believe it doesn't have to be because both parties can achieve tangible and immediate benefits from a mentoring relationship. I also believe that leaders who don't mentor do so at their peril.

Leaders are judged on their individual performance, but they're equally accountable for the performance of their direct reports. Even though C- and D-level performers may be great water cooler pals, they eventually drag the rest of the team down. By helping staff upgrade their skills, you're not "paying forward" anything. You're not doing a "good deed." You are doing the job for which you were hired. You're leading and developing leaders.

In my early corporate life, large companies tried to institutionalize the process of identifying and training potential top performers. Back then, promising new hires were recruited into an internal corporate management-training program. We spent our nights in pursuit of MBAs and our days mastering practical management and leadership skills, often under the supervision of an assigned mentor. Those who made the cut went on to become some of the top business leaders.

Those were great programs, and many of them still exist in some form. But can't we get even better at identifying and mentoring leaders? One approach might be to foster a system in which unconventional, off-the-grid minds are given access to leadership training reaching beyond corporate borders. Why not create a widespread series of programs in which the country's top talent can be identified as apprentice leaders and then encouraged to develop the skills they will need to succeed?

In the absence of established programs, junior managers need to mentor and teach *their* staff. It will help them grow as leaders and improve the team's performance.

When I became a CEO at Euro RSCG Becker, I began holding leadership classes and identifying those who seemed most open to learning and passionate about improving their performance. I thought of them as candidates for promotion and followed their progress closely, making it a point to chat with them periodically on leadership techniques. I made sure they received recognition when they deserved it and a reprimand when they were sloppy. I learned a lot from my personal role model, Jack Welch, and his books.

When you prepare to mentor, try to recall your own mentors. Chances are that you'll remember only a few words – but they were obviously ideas that made a big impression. Maybe they'll also be effective for you in your mentoring sessions.

As a young group product manager, I attended a talk by Bob Luciano, then President of Lederle Laboratories (now a part of Pfizer). Bob posed the following question to the audience – but I felt as if he were speaking directly to me: "What will be your legacy? When you hang it up, how do you want to be remembered?"

To many, this may have sounded like a platitude. Yet I've never forgotten those words and the inspiration they provided. In the years that followed, I've asked that question dozens of times in the course of mentorships. It doesn't always strike a chord, but when the person "gets" the idea, you'll see their face light up, as yours may have years before. And you'll have made a difference. Thank you, Bob.

ROLE MODELS

ONE OF MY "SECRETS" AS A PRODUCT MANAGER WAS finding great people to mentor me as I rose through the ranks and, in turn, mentoring my reports to help them hone their talents. My first personal role model was, of course, my mother Rose Flaum. I'll never forget when she said to me, "You'll have to work harder and be smarter than your competitors because you are a stutterer."

Jack Welch, businessman extraordinaire and stutterer, has had a profound influence on me. He took General Electric from number ten to number one and kept it at number one as long as he was CEO. Jack Welch, a stutterer who became an engineer because he didn't want to speak. After attaining his PhD at University of Chicago, he came back to GE as an engineer in Massachusetts. He went to a marketing meeting as part of his job, realized he really liked it, and decided he wanted to transition to the marketing department.

Someone from human resources said, "Jack, come on. You're a stutterer. You can't get into marketing."

He quit that day.

A couple of days later, human resources called him back, said, "Jack, we made a terrible mistake. If you come in, you will be in the marketing department starting Monday morning."

That was it.

Even with his disability, he moved up and up through the company and never stopped.

Clarence Page was on "The McLaughlin Report" when the show was live every Sunday morning. He is the Washington correspondent for *The Chicago Tribune*. He was also our emcee at the American Institute for the Stuttering gala in June. He stuttered every single Sunday morning while on live television. What a role model and hero.

My late wife, Mechele, was and remains my all-time hero for being a great advisor helping me deal with challenging clients and to cope with the superiors at Havas advertising. She helped me grow in my various roles and business ventures with her wise counsel.

TEACHING

I WORKED AS AN ADJUNCT professor of management at Fordham University Graduate School of Business for 16 years. I also chaired the Fordham Leadership Forum, where we brought in great CEOs in from all over to talk to the senior MBA students.

On the first day of class, I always made a point to say to my students, many of them foreign, that I am a stutterer and that I will have dysfluencies. I told them it's okay to *not* have perfect speech or speak in perfect English. My point to them (and what I really care about) is that *what* they have to say matters more than *how* they say it.

I understand how long and hard the work is to get to the point where you can speak in front of a group of strangers, or even people you may know well.

By the same token, I also spoke to my students about interviewing skills. These were young, bright, MBA students. I wanted them to get it right and get the jobs they wanted.

When I came to the part of how one dresses for interviews, I spoke to the men about proper grooming, haircut, nice suit, polished shoes, clean fingernails, writing thank you notes, etc. Then came to the women in class. I said the same thing, only I warned them against wearing too short a skirt on interviews. I said that no matter who is interviewing them, it might give the interviewer the wrong impression and to err on the side of a more conservative dress.

Unfortunately, my statement didn't take cultural sensitivities into account, and a female student from my class lodged a complaint against me for my comment. I was taken aback because I'd discussed this for over fourteen years and never had any of my female students pushed back. The complaint was turned over to the legal department and ultimately dismissed, but I felt badly that the student hadn't approached me directly to say I offended her. More damning was that neither the dean nor the president of the school had the courtesy to give me a call to tell me the complaint was dismissed with an apology.

In the aftermath however, we parted ways, and I retired from teaching.

TALK SHOW

MANY STUTTERERS HAVE DIFFERENT TECHNIQUES.
There's a group of five to ten people that meet every Wednesday
night at Starbucks on 39th Street and Broadway, practicing targets
and speaking to one another in conversation. My speech therapist
and speech pathologist friends tell me that "self-advertising" has
helped many of their clients over the years. Because the phone is a
death knell for stutterers, I keep a sign right in front of my phone
that reads, "Full breath and Amplitude Contour."

I took a workshop on public speaking to manage fear, anxiety, and other emotions that we all experience every time we have
to speak—stutterers and non-stutterers alike. I also started taking
a beta-blocker drug, which slows your heartbeat and helps calm
nerves which helps stuttering, at least for me. As a result, I was able
to do public speaking, interviews, presentations, some TV, and I
even did weekly radio show on PSR. It takes some work, but it is
worth it.

I had a radio show every week, every Tuesday morning called
The Leader's Edge on Public Service Radio in Connecticut. In order
to prep for that, I was in the gym in the morning at 5:45. I read

the scrolls on the TV sets, and I practiced my targets reading the scrolls, so I was fluent on my radio show. I did a talk about my speech disfluency on some of the radio shows. It sure helped.

BOOKS

I BEGAN TEACHING LEADERSHIP SKILLS AND ALSO
tried my hand at writing books. My first leadership book, *The 100-Mile Walk, was* co-authored with my son in 2005. As we strolled
the streets of New York and New Orleans, trekked through the
Blue Ridge Mountains, and hiked along the Long Island coast, we
talked about our experiences, our outlook on life and work, the
achievements of leaders we have known, and how we each viewed
the nature and purpose of leadership. The book, *The 100-Mile
Walk,* became a bestseller, and the process of writing exposed me to
a wider field of interests.

In 2009, I wrote, *Big Shoes: How Successful Leaders Grow into
New Roles* in response to the dearth of leadership accountability
evidenced around the world. My goal was to help new leaders and
managers faced with leadership challenges to think through their
first 100 days on the job and the days following with an eye to
build organizations and careers in which they could be proud.

*The Best Thing That Could Ever Happen to You: How A Career
Reversal Can Reinvigorate Your Life* was written in 2013 with the
help of Mechele and former senator John Glenn to get people

moving and into the job they've always wanted. Using tips and their proven methods, I showed readers how to conquer their fears and empower themselves again.

The Stutter Steps, which I published in 2021 with the help of Wes Smith and Heather Grossman Phd, CCC-SLP BCS-F is a departure from the business category and is intended to help stutterers and their caregiver with proven strategies, therapies, and real life success stories.

In 2022, I wrote *Benign Paranoia: The Sixth Sense that Keeps Leaders Ahead of the Pack* to share the secret the very best and the brightest CEOs, business leaders, and entrepreneurs rely upon ways to stay ahead of their competitors.

BOARDS, NON-PROFIT WORK AND ACCOMPLISHMENTS

I HAVE BROUGHT MY EXPERTISE TO VARIOUS companies as a member of the board. At The Ohio State University College of Arts and Sciences, I was named Executive Director at the Fisher College of Business and sponsor of the Flaum Speech Fluency Program as well. I am a board member of The John Glenn College of Public Affairs, The James Cancer Center, and the Dean's Advisory Board at Fairleigh Dickinson University, Silberman College of Business.

In addition, I have also served on the board of the American Friends of Tel Aviv University, a nonprofit organization that supports Israel's most influential, comprehensive, and sought-after center of higher learning, American Institute for Stuttering (AIS), where I served as the former Chairman of the Board of Directors, Dr. Ronald Webster's Hollins Communications Research Institute (HCRI), the advisory board for Marathon Pharmaceuticals, and LimeConnect, a not-for-profit organization that helps disabled college students find employment.

I was named one of the 2016 top healthcare transformers by *Medical Marketing & Media*, a monthly business publication for healthcare marketers. I was also honored by *PM360*, a monthly magazine for marketing decision makers in the pharmaceutical, biotech, and medical device industries as one of the top 100 most influential people in the healthcare industry in its 2nd Annual ELITE Awards in the Mentor category. I was recognized as one of the "100 Most Inspiring People" by PharmaVoice Magazine.

I was even chosen to be the commencement speaker at the Fordham Gabelli School of Business twice, in 2001 and 2010, and The Ohio State University Fisher College of Business in 2018. I was especially proud to have given each of these speeches without stuttering.

PHILANTHROPY

AFTER MY EXPERIENCE WITH HCRI, I BECAME AN advocate for others who stutter and made a commitment to make effective stuttering therapy more accessible. In 2009, I started the Rose Flaum Foundation, named after my mother, in 2009, to fund stuttering therapy scholarships to help individuals attend HCRI therapy and the American Institute for Stuttering. With an annual budget of $100,000, I grant tuition of up to $4,000 for those in need. The foundation gives money to many different charities that range from the ASPCA and Make-A-Wish to the speech related charities I'm proud to support.

It's crucial to help people financially and emotionally. I have always made it a point to ask people how they are doing and not to hear "fine" in return. I really wanted to know and be able to help if the answer is less than positive outcome. These days, a boss can't try and set up a lonely coworker or send a promising but poorly dressed young employee to Ralph Lauren with a clothing allowance so he can learn to dress the part.

While I'm well aware that I could be difficult and demanding to work for, I truly cared for and was there for my people. I hope my philanthropy has succeeded in reaching many people whom I will never meet. It has been one of my primary life goals to make a difference.

PART IV
WALKING THE WALK

AN UNBEARABLE LOSS

MECHELE AND I ENJOYED NEARLY TWO DECADES OF happiness together before she was stricken with ovarian cancer in 2009. It was a horrible shock. We were able to get it into remission for a while with good medications, but the cancer came back. We went to every major cancer center in New York, New York, and Massachusetts and tried all the new medications available.

I encouraged her to go to different doctors and try whatever treatments were out there. I really didn't believe she would succumb to the disease.

When she said no more, they gave her three weeks to live. She passed one week later.

It's been nearly six years, and I sometimes still have trouble believing it's true.

It's been an enormous loss for me and for so many others.

I honestly never realized how charitable she was until she passed away. She served on the boards of the Women's Campaign International, Women's Executive Circle of the United Jewish Federation, the Global Organization for Organ Donation, the Doe Fund, and the Brooklyn Friends School, but it wasn't until I got her checkbook until I realized just how many people and charities she also was helping.

The New York Times had a Fresh Air program where you could sponsor foster children for summer experiences out of the city. Mechele wanted children, but I didn't, so every summer we took two sisters in the foster care system to stay at our house on Kellis Pond in the Hamptons for two weeks. We invited them so that their visit could coincide with our annual Fourth of July party. Mechele not only wanted them to experience a different world but supported them so they could create one for themselves by setting up trusts in their names which survive to this day. My wife was instrumental in helping these girls lead successful lives as adults.

I was by her side when my darling, Mechele Flaum, died at our home in Manhattan on Nov. 10, 2017.

I like to believe she is driving around in her perfectly restored 1971 white convertible, a Ford Torino, and warmed by heavenly sunshine.

CHILDREN, GRANDCHILDREN, AND FAMILY

ONE OF THE BIGGEST MISTAKES I MADE DURING MY climb to the top of the corporate ladder was not finding that work/life balance. I did not find enough time to spend with my children while they were growing up, and it my damaged relationships with them. The time I did spend with them was more for discipline and less for simply having fun together.

My son, Jonathon, recalls how hurt he was by the fact that I was the only father that never attended any of this baseball games – not one. I recall speaking to a colleague about raising children while trying to grow a company. I jokingly commented that while my eldest, Pamela, was growing up, I believe there were nine words spoken between us, six of which were not good.

It wasn't funny.

I have since mended the fences with both of my children. The choices we make as parents have long-term effects on our children.

Jonathon lives in Asheville, North Carolina. He is married with two wonderful children. He is a great writer and helped me pen my first book and now is an executive at the famed Biltmore Hotel in Asheville.

Pamela is a major coach for women who decided to go back to work after having a family. Her two children are very successful. The youngest works for his dad at a wealth management company. Rebecca is an associate producer for a major TV talk show organization.

Mechele and I had a deal with the grandchildren that when they read bat or bar mitzvah, we would take them anywhere in the world with us. Our oldest grandchild had a dream to go to Paris, so we made all the reservations and really got to see Paris and France with her. We had a great time. She still says it's the best vacation she's ever had.

My sister Adele grew up to become the assistant principal of a Hebrew school with campuses in Manhattan and Long Island.

When it was time, paid for my father to go to assisted living. Adele and I alternated visiting him every week. Paid for clothing, rent etc., and took care of him, despite it all.

I DID IT AND SO CAN YOU

MY SON COMPARED ME TO SISYPHUS, who according to Greek myth, spent eternity trying to roll a giant boulder up a hill. Stuttering has been my boulder, my greatest challenge.

He suggested at one point that mediation might help me be gentler and accepting of myself. He taught me the basics, but like anything, it takes practice. Relaxing and clearing my mind doesn't come naturally. Eventually, I learned how to calm my mind and body. Everyone must find what works best for them. I'll never be able to meditate at the level of a maharishi or a monk, but I have found a method that helps considerably.

Meditation and mindfulness were once considered "far out," but now they are widely practiced in corporate America and around the world.

In order to apply meditation to stuttering, I take a few minutes to meditate by clearing my mind of all distractions. I do this by practicing breathing exercises that slow down my heartrate. I then focus my thinking on memories or images that make me feel peaceful and secure.

This is the simple way I clear my mind for meditation: I hold my favorite pen in my hand. I put both feet flat on the ground, close my eyes, and take slow breaths in and out. Then I think about all the stuff I've written with that pen. This clears my mind and relaxes me.

Meditation is considered the formal practice of mindfulness, according to the speech therapists at AIS and Hollins—both of whom incorporate meditation and mindfulness into their therapeutic programs. When I meditate on a regular basis, it helps reduce my anxiety about stuttering, which in turn, helps me speak more fluently. Mindfulness and meditation help foster a "calm awareness" of what is happening inside the mind and outside the body.

Speech pathologists and researchers in the field have found that mindfulness meditation can be life-changing for those whose stutter. While they warn that it is not a cure-all, there are many who believe the benefits are considerable and maybe even "life-changing."

For me, it helps. I have a need to learn something new every day—the need to have a competitive edge all the time. If I can't learn something new, I become a little depressed.

I'm a lot older, and a little wiser, but the issues are still the same! The biggest issue is—are you going to feel sorry for yourself when you have a painful speech day? Are you going to become depressed, beat yourself up, and going to say, "Why me?" Or will you continue to move on and work a little harder and smarter than anyone else and get people to think about *what* not you say, not *how* you say it?

Those of us in corporate life know that sometimes you get one shot at the board. You make one presentation, and you are judged for the rest of your career by that moment. I am hopeful, too, that one benefit of being in the new and more diverse global economy is that people are much more accepting of all speech impediments… accents, lisps, and other speech handicaps.

Many of the people who stutter I've known actually believe that stuttering has helped make them a better, more compassionate, more interesting, and more determined person.

I try to follow these 10 steps for transforming adversity to inspiration:

1. Start Small: Find one thing you love, and stay close to it daily. Be it sewing, fishing, or meditation, if it's helped you before, go to it now, and do it daily.

2. Keep Walking: Stagnation keeps you stuck. Let the adversity move through you. This literally means to "walk it off." Be outside walking daily, rain or shine, or hear or cold — follow the mailman code; it will deliver you.

3. Understand the facts of what happened; don't settle for your self-defeating story of blame. Get a therapist to help you if necessary.

4. Be with Friends who Care: Adversity is too difficult to process alone; ask for help.

5. Find a spiritual practice that works for you: Self-reliance isn't enough. Now is a time for community and wider deeper meaning.

6. Get in Nature: The Japanese coined the term "forest bathing" as a means to lower stress, blood pressure, and heighten mood. Nature inspires, so get out in it.

7. Leave behind the thing that is no longer serving you, be it job, relationship, or residence. Make a fresh start.

8. Get away for two weeks to a place you've never been before: Exploration and new experiences allow you to see yourself and your life differently.

9. Learn a new skill: tennis, scuba diving, whatever. Just get out of your head and old habits. New activities and motions produce new ideas about yourself.

10. Detach from your former identity: Who are you now? Find out.

After these ten steps, you'll be able to forge a new life post adversity. It is the scariest and most exciting thing you will ever do.

My stuttering will always be the *crucible experience,* which will always keep me sharp and prepared to do whatever I do next, beyond expectations. I must be fluent, practice my targets, and stay fluent every day, or else it's a distraction to my clients, so I think about this impediment in a constant way.

People listen to you, so you can't be ordinary. You can't be mediocre. For the rest of your life—every minute, every hour, every day—you need to be better than the competition. There's no letting up.

Never give up. It can be done.

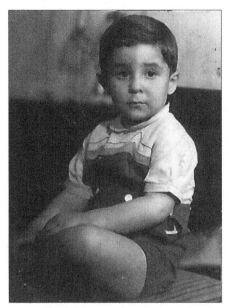

Sander Flaum 1940

Spring 1945: My Mother Rose, sister Adele, and me in our new suite

US Army buddies, 1961, Fort Drum, NY.
I'm the handsome one with his hands in his pockets

April 1982: Flaum Appetizers, Brooklyn, NY

Senator John Glenn and me at OSU speaking to the stuttering students in 2000

2006 Business Week did an interview with Sander about his new book,
The 100-Mile Walk

May 2015: From Left to Right Me, Dr. Rheta "Rookie" Hirsch,
Dr. Bob Marmer, Norm "the bear" Pessin, David Braverman and Stan Gelber

Senator Joe Biden and I chaired a committee together at
John Glenn College of Public Affairs in 2018

PM360 Magazine did an interview on Sander Flaum receiving the
lifetime achievement award

PM360 Magazine in 2018 on a day in the life of Sander Flaum including him
recording his weekly radio show, The Leader's Edge on Robinhood Radio

Spring of 1988 when Mechele and I were dating

For Mechele's birthday, Sander surprised Mechele with a plaque placed on the bench they liked to sit on in Central Park in 2007

Oct 2001: Mechele and me over the years we had a lot of fun together

OSU game

Rome, Italy

July 4 party at our house

Made in the USA
Middletown, DE
25 September 2022

10849302R00080